The
Diane Keaton
Scrapbook

The Diane Keaton Scrapbook

by Suzanne Munshower

Publishers · GROSSET & DUNLAP · New York
A FILMWAYS COMPANY

Copyright © 1979 by Suzanne Munshower
All rights reserved
Published simultaneously in Canada
Library of Congress catalog card number: 78-067808
ISBN: 0-448-16380-2
First printing 1979
Printed in the United States of America

Contents

For Pam, who never had a bicycle

Beginnings

She's the la-di-da girl, the hesitantly smiling beauty who started a worldwide fashion trend when she walked on-screen in her baggy clothes in *Annie Hall,* the neurotic schoolteacher who got bludgeoned to death after one too many pickups in *Looking for Mr. Goodbar,* the real-life actress whom pal Woody Allen calls one of the greatest comediennes in the world.

She's Diane Keaton, who refers to herself as an "aging child," and who insists that, as much as she likes being an actress, she'd rather be a successful singer any day.

What is Diane Keaton really like? She's a one-woman study in contrasts. A consummate actress, she's still amazed that other people appreciate her talent, that she's a big draw at the box office. A slender wraith of a woman, she defines her fashion sense as "eclectic" and dresses in a startling style that belies her genuine shyness. A self-confessed wallflower in high school, she's gone from living with the less-than-Barrymore-ish Woody Allen to dating the undeniably super-handsome Warren Beatty. Often she defies understanding, and she's quick to admit that she's sometimes rather puzzled herself.

When she speaks, Diane conveys immediate warmth. She punctuates her speech with laughter, sometimes heartfelt, sometimes nervous and hesitant. Though Diane goes to great lengths to make her views clear, she's considered a difficult interview because of her tendency to leave sentences dangling, to change trains of thought in the middle of the track, to leave a thought hanging indefinitely while she mulls over the right word to express her feelings.

Feelings are important to Diane, certainly much more important than words. She's not glib or polished, but anyone who

Diane has always sported the "Annie Hall" look, even back in 1976, when this picture was taken.

takes the time to listen to what she has to say quickly learns that a great deal of careful thought lies behind every remark.

Diane has parlayed her lack of verbal finesse, her vulnerable uncertainty, into great success as an actress. She's won a huge following by putting much of herself into her roles. The parts she played in Woody's films—spaced-out but well-meaning heroines—made her an audience favorite. Her work in the films of other directors—movies like *The Godfather* and *Looking for Mr. Goodbar*—has shown that she's capable of portraying more a blood-and-guts type of woman, even though she keeps audiences aware of the sensitivity and gentleness that is the key to understanding any of the characters she plays.

Still, despite her success and popularity, self-confidence has never been her strong suit. When Diane played Al Pacino's wife in the original version of *The Godfather*, she received only $6,000 for her work, the biggest woman's role in the film. Even after she was a star, Diane insisted she hadn't been underpaid for that job. "I was delighted to get it," she said in all modesty. "After all, who am I?"

Who is she? Today, as the result of beating out such established actresses as Anne Bancroft, Shirley MacLaine, Jane Fonda, and Marsha Mason in the 1977 Oscar race, Diane Keaton is one of the most sought after leading ladies in motion pictures. She can pick and choose her roles. She is deluged with scripts. She rates a place on the "A" list for parties. She's a star, though an eccentric one. Diane Keaton has come a long way from her all-American, Southern California background.

Diane had what could be called a typical California childhood. Certainly her past wasn't filled with traumas. She was (and still thinks of herself as) an L.A. girl through and through. Diane admits that the character she played in *Annie Hall* was based upon her real-life personality, and, in fact, her real last name *is* Hall. She was born Diane Hall in Los Angeles on January 5, 1946, the eldest of four children, to parents who belonged to California's manicured middle class. Her father, Jack, is a well-to-do engineer and real-estate broker. These days he heads his own consulting firm. Her mother, Dorothy is a talented semiprofessional photographer who once won a Mrs. Los Angeles contest.

Diane took her mother's maiden name when she started acting professionally, and so far she's the only one of the Hall children to choose show business as a career. Her only brother, Randy, works with his father in the family business. Sister Robin is a nurse, and sister Dorrie is a recent college graduate who seems disinclined to follow her sister's footsteps into the acting field.

What made Diane choose acting as a career? Maybe it was just the proximity of Hollywood during her childhood. Certainly, she showed neither the natural gift nor the neurotic tendencies that have characterized many children who long to be stars. Her childhood was pretty uneventful, both in Los Angeles and in Santa Ana, where the Halls moved when Diane was ten.

You can't find a more wholesome-looking place in America than Orange County, and Santa Ana is very much of that county.

Diane grew up as a typical, wholesome California girl. Today you're more likely to find her prowling the streets of New York than surrounded with this suburban splendor.

Above: Diane was thrilled to bring her youngest sister, Dorrie, to the 1977 Academy Awards presentation, during which she won an Oscar for *Annie Hall*.

That happy-looking woman in back of Diane is her mother, who's very proud of her daughter's success.

Right: Oscar winners Diane Keaton and Richard Dreyfuss are representatives of the new wave of film stars. They're intelligent young actors who are making America want to return to the movies.

Orange County is a celebrated right-wing stronghold, a sprawling group of communities whose teenagers look more like Donny and Marie Osmond than punk rockers. But something in Diane's apple-pie childhood made her want to be different.

The only unusual thing Diane can recall about herself as a child is her love of singing. "I've wanted to be a singer ever since I was five years old," she confesses. "I just never thought I wanted to be a star."

It was singing that propelled Diane into a childhood interest in theatricals, singing that put her in the spotlight at home. She vividly remembers singing to the moon. "It was a way of getting attention from my mother and father because they were really thrilled whenever I would do any of this kind of thing," she explains, "and it always seemed to be the only thing I could do." So little Diane Hall sang, mostly to the accompaniment of Judy Garland or Doris Day records. She avoided the records of male singers because she felt she couldn't really sing along with them.

Singing was Diane's first love, and it was as a singer that she made her stage debut in the ninth grade, in the school's talent show. Diane blacked out her front teeth and sang "All I Want for Christmas Is My Two Front Teeth" with another girl.

This may not have been an auspicious debut, but it did give Diane a good dose of stagitis. After her initial taste of applause, she went after it full speed ahead. By her senior year, she was one of her school's more established actresses, snagging the second lead in its production of *Little Mary Sunshine.*

In spite of her forays onto center stage,

Diane says she wasn't especially motivated to be an actress in high school. As a teenager, she was less goal-oriented and more boy-oriented than some of her fellow students. She remembers being heavily into makeup, partial to the whitish shades of lipstick and dark eye makeup in vogue in the late fifties and early sixties. She was clothes-conscious, too, tending toward tight skirts more than the baggies favored by Annie Hall.

Most of all, Diane remembers her high school days as revolving around boys. She dreamed of dating basketball players even as she spent her evenings with boys shorter than she was. She wanted to be a *femme fatale* "though I never had much success getting dates. I just couldn't concentrate on English and geography and math, but I jumped right into the singing and drama groups. Even there, the big thing was to make everyone *like* me. I still remember playing Blanche in *A Streetcar Named Desire* in our drama class, and do you know something? I had no idea—no *idea*—of what that play was all about."

Diane was then slightly overweight, though she couldn't have been called fat. She was popular without being the prom queen type, attractive without being beautiful. She certainly didn't seem destined for greatness as she sold popcorn at a Santa Ana theater. She didn't have the colossal drive or the overwhelming ambition others of her generation displayed, but she did have the quiet determination to keep on plugging and to make something of herself. By the time she graduated from high school, Diane Keaton was on her way to success as an actress.

The Big Break

Diane never really considered doing anything but acting for a living. She wasn't fervent about her dramatic interests, but she *was* steady. She attended two different colleges—Santa Ana College for one semester and Orange Coast College for just a couple of months—and today says she didn't learn much at either institution. It was the head of her high school drama department who steered her away from a liberal arts college education and toward New York City.

The drama coach advised a course of study at Sanford Meisner's respected Neighborhood Playhouse School of the Theater. Diane asked her parents for permission to quit college and go to Manhattan. Jack and Dorothy Hall promptly bundled their whole brood into a Ford van and drove east to check things out. The school, and the idea of Diane's living in New York, met with their approval. And Diane met with the approval of the Neighborhood Playhouse. In 1965, she started studying at the school on a scholarship.

Diane didn't find immediate success in New York, but then, not many aspiring actresses or actors do. She studied hard and worked as a hatcheck girl to support herself. Then she did what young actresses waiting for a break usually do—she went on the road in summer stock. After returning to New York, she went for long periods without work. Times were lean when she auditioned for *Hair.* Along with many others, she was rejected.

What seemed like a low point in her career miraculously turned into that all-important break. "I went out to the elevator," she remembers, "and, man, did I feel bad. I mean, I felt bad. I was thinking, 'This is ridiculous.' Then along came one of the producers, this French guy, and he said, 'No, you stay.' I have no idea why he

John R. Hamilton/Globe Photos

decided to keep me.''

It was a lucky decision for Diane, since she ended up replacing the lead, Lynn Kellogg, who was leaving the show. *Hair* was in the news at the time because of its nude finale. Even in the late sixties nudity in the theater was considered quite daring, though one could hardly accuse the *Hair* cast of arousing anyone's ''prurient interest.'' At the end of the show, as they stood in a circle of muted lighting, various cast members unobtrusively removed their clothes and remained naked onstage. It was sort of a hippie-ish statement on the beauty of nature, and the stripping was done strictly on a volunteer basis. Different performers took off their clothes on different nights, going with the mood of the moment and getting naked whenever they felt like it. Except for Diane. Diane never felt like it. It wasn't long before she became known as the girl who wouldn't take her clothes off.

Her decision to remain clothed wasn't a bad career move, since it certainly garnered her more publicity than the clothes-shedders got. But it wasn't a calculated attention-getting device. Diane just didn't feel like doing that onstage.

Several years later, she still felt the same way. On the subject of nudity, she told a reporter from the New York *Daily News*, ''The only thing I'm opposed to is me doing it. I'm so shy and self-conscious about my body, I like to be clothed. But I don't mind viewing nudity. It depends on what it is. I went to a porno film about a year ago, and I couldn't sit through all of it. Not only was it not funny, it was pretty strange, come to think of it.''

Diane (who confesses she sneaked an oc-casional peak at the undressed cast members sharing the stage with her) stayed with *Hair* for nine months. Then something happened that was to prove very important to her future. She heard that auditions were being held for comedian Woody Allen's first stage venture, *Play It Again, Sam*.

After thinking it over carefully, Diane decided to audition for Allen's play. *Hair* wsa a very successful show that would un-doubtedly run for quite a while, but Diane wanted something more. *Hair* stressed en-semble acting and singing. It wasn't a vehicle for displaying individual talents. Diane wanted to be in a show that had a meatier part for her.

When Diane showed up for the *Play It Again, Sam* auditions, she was far from an established actress—or even an especially successful one. If anyone had told her a successful comic like Woody Allen would be petrified of her, she wouldn't have be-lieved it. But it was true.

Woody was intimidated by Diane at their first meeting. As he recalls it, ''She was a Broadway star, and who was I? A cabaret comedian who had never even been on a stage before.''

Woody then was just like Woody now—minus the confidence he's acquired from years of fame and success. He planned to play the lead role in his new show, a nebbish in love with the wife of his best friend. When the couple has problems, Woody goes after the girl himself, trying to be cool and visualizing himself as Hum-phrey Bogart even as he makes one *faux pas* after another.

Diane ended up with the female lead. Tony Roberts played the husband (today

Diane and Woody appear in a scene from the 1972 film, *Play It Again, Sam*.

St. Francis Hotel

PICCADILLY

17

he's Woody's real-life best friend as well), and Jerry Lacy played the Bogart persona. For Diane and Woody, it was the start of a lasting and important relationship.

Of that first audition, Diane says, "I have a vivid memory of that day. Woody had to come up on the stage and walk round and round with me, since one of the major concerns was to see whether or not I would be too tall for him. I was absolutely astonished to find that Woody was more frightened of me than I was of him."

If Diane had been five-foot-nine, the course of film history might have been different. As it was, her five feet seven inches made her only three-quarters of an inch taller than Woody. That slight difference didn't make Woody overly self-conscious, and Diane got the job.

During the run of the show, she got the man as well. She, Woody, and Tony Roberts immediately became fast friends. After all, they were spending most of their nights together, and several of their days. Propinquity bred romance.

During the run of the show, Diane and Woody started living together. He was thirty-three and she was twenty-two. The short, slight, bespectacled Jewish boy and the tall, slim WASP princess responded to something in each other than created magic on the stage and off it.

The initial phase of their relationship was much like the love story Woody put on the screen years later in *Annie Hall*. They didn't meet playing tennis, as they did in the film, but each was in awe of the other. And Diane, Woody insists, was just as spacey as any of the characters she's played in his films.

In *Play It Again, Sam* Dick and Linda (Tony Roberts and Diane Keaton) try to find the perfect date for Woody.

Not that Woody ever considered Diane dumb. It was just, he says, that when he met her, "her mind was completely blank." She was Diane Hall from Orange County, California, nurtured on wholesomeness and mindlessness, a stranger to the classics, to deep philosophical study, to intense psychological probing. On the other hand, Woody was Allen Stewart Konigsberg from Brooklyn, who'd loved baseball as a kid, but who had also wondered about the meaning of death while he was still losing his baby teeth. They were true opposites in most ways. Only in their mutual insecurity, their twin senses of inferiority, did they seem alike.

"When I first met her," Woody reminisces, "she was a real hayseed, the kind who would chew eight sticks of gum at a time. I talked to her on the phone once when she was in California and she was about to drive to the supermarket—which was across the street. *Literally.* Very California."

She was very California; he was very New York. Something clicked between them almost immediately. With their co-star Tony Roberts, Woody and Diane quickly formed a triumvirate of buddies. The three would hang out together constantly, frequently going to Woody's favorite restaurant, Elaine's, after the show for some Italian food and convivial conversation, catching the Knicks' games whenever they could fit them into their schedules (Woody is one of the all-time great sports fans), and, in general, just having a good time together. Diane would often keep the two men in hysterics with her wry comments and her offbeat way of

Tony Roberts met Diane when they both starred on stage in *Play It Again, Sam*. They're still good friends.

© Robin Platzer, Images

Maybe he isn't an Adonis, but plenty of women think Woody Allen's got sex appeal.

looking at things. It wasn't so much what she said as how she said it. Woody, with his trained ear and comedic bent, realized from the start that Diane was a natural, that she had an innate flair for making things funny.

It has been reported more than once that before Diane met Woody, she had remarked that she thought he looked "like a mole." She herself refuses to believe that she ever uttered that phrase.

John R. Hamilton/Globe Photos

Sleeper, 1973,
both on and off camera.

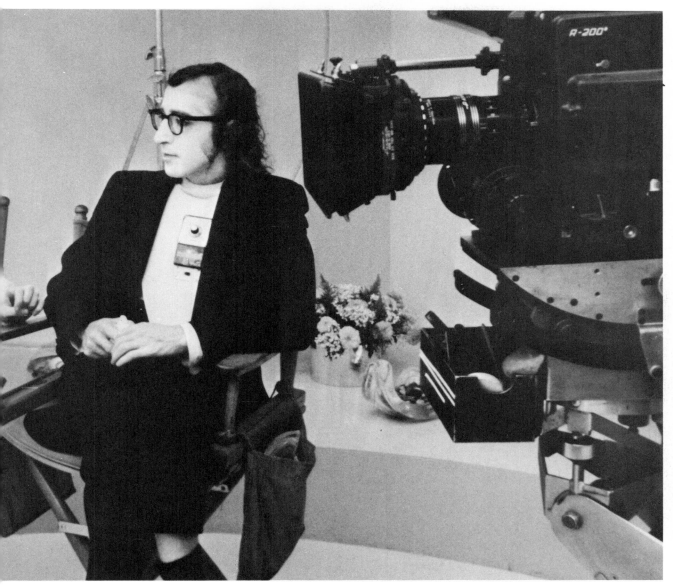

"I don't remember saying that!" she insists. "I don't think he looks like a mole! I've always thought he was kind of cute. Gorgeous men always put me off. I think in my life I've only had one gorgeous boyfriend. One. But when you get to know someone very well, his face changes."

In any case, it certainly wasn't Allen's looks that attracted Diane. He was unlike anyone she'd come across in Southern California. He was an intellectual, a serious-minded man who had devoted his life to educating himself and who was resolved to attack important philosophical questions through the mode of comedy.

Still, if Woody has always been a talented comic, he has never been a lighthearted, casual wit. He was immediately drawn to Diane's inherent zaniness, to her natural flair for the comedic. "Diane was just born funny," he's said. "She can take a perfectly straight paragraph and read it and you'll be rolling on the floor. She has unfailing good taste. Her mind is never clouded by popular opinion, the need to score points. I can show her something and say the two greatest writers in the world love it, and she can pick it up and say, 'I don't know what's so great about this.' And she'll be right."

Woody's professional and personal interest in Diane has had an effect on the rest of us. If Diane and Woody hadn't gotten together in a friendship that was to prove important to them both, movie audiences might never have had the chance to fall in love with the scatterbrained, well-meaning character Woody presented to the world in the person of Diane.

Diane and Woody ride the rapids in *Sleeper*.

Movies, Movies, Movies

Woody Allen has been *the* major force in Diane's career. But she's quick to bristle at the suggestion that he's been the only one. Because her most memorable screen roles so far have been in Allen's movies, Diane has been hit time and again with the suggestion that she might not have made it as an actress if Woody Allen hadn't entered her life.

Diane resents those implications, and rightly so. When asked by the *New York Times* if she thought she owed her career to Allen, Diane told them, "I wouldn't say that. Things in life happen. I hope there would be a way for me to work without having met him. I'd have to say that I think I'd be able to work without him."

Woody doesn't have to be defensive. After all, he was an established talent way before he met Keaton. No one is ever going to accuse him of having ridden on her coattails to success. So it's not surprising that he sings her praises, saying, "Diane has been my lucky charm. She came out of the boondocks of Southern California, completely guileless. She sees directly to the reality of a thing. When I made my first movie, *Take the Money and Run*, I felt I had struck out. I didn't even know how to show a rough cut. I'd show it at eleven o'clock at night to fifteen soldiers from the USO and it had crayon marks and splice marks all over it and nobody was laughing at all. But I showed it to her and she said, 'This is funny,' and she was right. And since then she's been a consistently clear mind and clear voice on every picture I've made."

Many people are unaware of just how many non-Woody projects Diane has pursued. This is probably because her roles in them have never garnered the praise that her parts in Allen's movies have. After

Diane with Michael Caine in *Harry and Walter Go to New York*, 1976.

leaving the stage version of *Play It Again, Sam*, Diane found herself with time on her hands before filming (with the original stage cast) was to begin, so she made a series of television commercials.

The commercials (she did three altogether) were for a deodorant and called for her to be a sweating housewife jogging around her kitchen in a track suit. Of the various commercials she did over the years, Diane admits, "I didn't care to do them, but they made money. I didn't find them fun." She remembers getting $25,000 for each of her track suit appearances.

Diane's non-Woody Allen pictures include *Lovers and Other Strangers*, *Harry and Walter Go to New York*, *I Will, I Will . . . for Now*, both *Godfather* features, and *Looking for Mr. Goodbar*.

Diane has been called "invisible" in the *Godfather* pictures, and it's true that her roles in both were pretty uninspired. In the original *Godfather*, as Michael Corleone's WASP girlfriend Kay, her role consisted mostly of asking Al Pacino questions about the rest of his family—especially about his father, the infamous Godfather (played by Marlon Brando).

By the time of *Godfather II*, she had married Corleone. One critic claimed she spent all her screen time rebuking Pacino for killing people and telling him he should be spending more time with their kids. She had a traditional woman's role in an action movie, and there wasn't anything especially rewarding about it.

Keaton herself sums up *Godfather II* with, "Pacino was great. Robert De Niro was great. I was background music."

In the first *Godfather* film, Diane never

understood what she was supposed to be doing. She felt she didn't belong in the movie, and her image of herself as an outsider stayed with her from start to finish. She recalls, "I tested with Al Pacino, Jimmy Caan, and Marty Sheen. They weren't really interested in me. They were interested in getting a Michael Corleone. And when they took me for the wife part, I couldn't see it."

Shy, insecure Diane was far from at ease on the set. Among the predominantly male cast of *The Godfather*, she remembers feeling "so inconsequential and all I could do was be very friendly and very nice and very scared. Jeeze, every time I'd run into Marlon Brando on the set, my face would turn red and I'd start laughing. I was so *high school*. So totally into self-loathing."

In all her Woody-less films, Diane was personally well reviewed, but most of the movies were less than interesting. She starred in *I Will, I Will . . . for Now* with Elliott Gould, an admirer who says Diane has the personality of "an Amish groupie." The film was just another tepid domestic comedy, à la Doris Day and Rock Hudson, but Diane was wonderful as the wife. *Harry and Walter Go to New York* was a hodgepodge of various themes. It was an attempt to cash in on both the "buddy" and the caper films rather than a cohesive motion picture. Diane was wonderful in her supporting role, but she was at sea in the whole thing, as were her co-stars, Elliott Gould, James Caan, and Michael Caine.

Diane did have a good role in a good movie—the part of Richard Castellano's reserved daughter-in-law who throws him into a panic by deciding to divorce his son

Diane enlivened the complex caper of *Harry and Walter Go to New York* with her own comic charm. Here she poses with Elliott Gould and James Caan.

in *Lovers and Other Strangers*. But that movie was filled with small roles performed by able actors, and Diane was just one of many talented people shining in it.

One of the best things Keaton has done as an actress was her portrayal of the night school teacher in Israel Horowitz's play, *The Primary English Class*. In it, she played an eager young teacher giving instruction in English as a second language, only to find that no one in her class speaks English at all, and that no two students speak the same tongue. In a beautifully orchestrated piece of characterization, Diane's young schoolteacher goes from nervous willingness, to blossoming panic, to bigoted name-calling and rage. She was onstage almost every minute of the play and proved to any doubting critics that she was a fine actress who could acquit herself admirably before a live audience in a small, intimate theater.

There's no denying, of course, that Diane's work in Woody's films has been her most notable, or at least, her most noticeable. Allen has not been the only force in her career, but he's certainly been the prime force in making her a bona fide star. Through her roles in his films, Diane has become an audience favorite. More than the other actresses who have co-starred with him—actresses like Jennifer Salt and Louise Lasser—Diane has been the perfect foil for Woody's offbeat brand of comedy. On-screen, the two balance each other and create a special kind of energy.

Of course, until *Interiors* (her first post-*Mr. Goodbar* movie with Woody), the characters Diane played in Allen's films were more dizzy than brainy. In *Sleeper*,

The Godfather II — a family portrait.

Diane as she appeared in *The Godfather* with Al
Pacino.

her character was so dense that she
couldn't repeat even one simple sentence
of instructions without messing it up. She
was Woody's girl of the future, wide-eyed
and silly, a surface intellectual unmasked
by his character as the scatterbrained chick
she really was. Her Sonia in *Love and
Death* was in the same mold, pretentiously
inclined to discuss abstract philosophical
concepts, but incapable of understanding
them. Her real motivation seemed to be
sexual. Like so many of Allen's female
characters, Sonia was happy as a housewife, though as inept at that job as she was
at any other. As Jennifer Salt in *Take the
Money and Run* lovingly served her husband (Woody) a broiled steak still in its
singed cellophane wrapper, so Diane as
Sonia served her spouse (Woody again) a
variety of dishes fabricated from snow.

In *Annie Hall*, Diane plays a character
with more dimensions. Since that film is
more realistic than Allen's previous films,
she portrays a real person for a change.

Diane attended the 1974 Academy Awards with her *Godfather* co-star, Al Pacino. She felt she was lost in the movie.

And since so much of the story is based on the real relationship between Diane and Woody, the two connect on-screen in *Annie Hall* much more than they do in their other films together. There's a real magic when Diane and Woody are joking or walking or talking together. Even in the smallest scenes, such as the one where the two are cooking lobsters, there's a sense of the magic between them.

Both Woody and Diane admit that *Annie Hall* is based on their real relationship.

And Woody has not given himself any breaks in his interpretation of the breakdown of the relationship. It's a movie made with love, a Valentine of sorts to Diane Keaton, and it's this genuine warmth and heartfelt emotion that distinguishes it from Woody's other films.

As is obvious from a viewing of *Annie Hall*, Woody Allen is not a man who is easy to live with. He's been in analysis for twenty-three of his forty-three years and shows no signs of dropping out. All these years of self-examination have been shared with his audiences. By re-creating his doubts and worries on the screen, he has managed to turn modern neuroses into an art form. In his latest film, the stark, *Interiors*, he has established himself as a writer/director who's captured the angst, terror, and uncertainty of the late-seventies in America.

In real life, Woody Allen embraces his neuroses with fervor. He is fascinated by the convolutions and complications of his own psyche, and one surmises that he has remained in analysis for so long because he admires and appreciates psychotherapy as an art form.

Speaking on the subject of his analysis not long ago, Woody admitted to an interviewer, "I knew it was going to take some time, maybe three, four, five years. But I thought when that time was over, then I could play the piano. I had an unrealistic expectation that I would not have any real neurotic problems. Maybe I haven't been able to part with many anxieties because they are common to everybody. In a certain sense, I'm not at all neurotic."

Though he may consider himself as normal as a twenty-four-hour day, Allen also appreciates himself as a hotbed of complexities. He is currently seeing his third analyst, a woman, and he says that one reason he remains in such intensive self-contemplation is for the sake of his work as an artist, feeling that "if I lost some of these anxieties, I'd be able to reach more of humanity with my work. A comedian like W. C. Fields, who was an enormous comic talent, spoke to a smaller audience because there was a certain lack of personal integration, a certain neurotic quality, whereas Chaplin had a greater feeling for the human condition."

As all this indicates, Woody isn't a laugh a minute. Far from it. He's an extremely serious man, and proud of that serious bent. Some of his critical admirers think that Woody doesn't respect himself enough as a comic. It's almost as if he feels he won't be taken seriously by the most important people unless he stops playing it for laughs, and a picture like *Interiors* is what he's been aiming for through his entire career. *Interiors* is so unrelievedly serious that one imagines Woody wanted to make sure that no one could possibly accuse him of straying into the familiar field of comedy with *this* movie.

Allen approaches everything with earnestness. Watching him play the clarinet in Michael's Pub in Manhattan, one is aware of the pride he takes in being a purist. Unlike many jazz musicians, Woody neither slouches nor drifts off. Instead, he sits straight in his chair in the best Preservation Hall Jazz Band style, sticking strictly to established Dixieland form.

As a literary man, Woody is definitely of a serious bent. He chose to curl up with *Conversations with Carl Jung* rather than attend the 1977 Academy Awards, and admirers of his work cite his *New Yorker* pieces (of which he himself is justifiably proud) as his finest work. These short pieces are masterpieces of satire, on a par with the best work of Robert Benchley and S. J. Perelman. His prose is incisive and cutting, his imagery unforgettable. And, like most truly intellectual artists, he is constantly preoccupied with making his

I Will, I Will . . . For Now
was passed over by the
critics as a tepid roman-
tic comedy. Nevertheless,
Diane was marvelous as
Elliott Gould's co-star.

ideas comprehensible and entertaining. Comedy is the form he's managed to use best in doing this.

Woody Allen sees the serious side of every lighthearted comment, the dark side of the brightest moon in the evening sky. He is always aware that the good times end, that death lurks at the end of the line, that pain is the nether side of pleasure. *Love and Death* is the most apt title of any of Woody's movies because it names the two things he's most preoccupied with.

Love is one of the major themes in all his work. He is enthralled by the beauty of relationships, and yet anxious in the knowledge that they can end at any moment. The interaction of men and women has long interested him, and with *Annie Hall* and *Interiors,* he's attempted to deal more seriously with his feelings and questions on this subject.

Death is a constant reference in his prose and films. Few works by Woody get by without at least one mention of the Grim Reaper, and in *Love and Death,* we see the ultimate fantasy of the Woody character—dead, dancing merrily off into the sunset with the specter of Death itself.

Woody sees mortality lurking around every corner, taking the edge off every moment of pleasure. "I was watching Walt Frazier one night with the Knicks," he told *Newsweek.* "He was so beautiful and young, so dazzling, but I saw the death's-head looming. I thought of the inevitable deterioration, the waning away of the adulation. I felt that anger and rage, not at anything correctable, but at the human condition that you're part of, too. I was with Keaton, and leaving the Garden I had that underground-man feeling, the decay at the core of existence. So I'm no fun to be with at parties because I'm very aware of this all the time."

Woody isn't the average "good catch," but he's obviously a very sensitive and aware man. Girls watch him adoringly at Michael's Pub and try to pass him notes and phone numbers, women mob him when they see his familiar figure in its plaid shirt and khaki slacks on the street, and females of all ages stand in line for hours to watch him on the screen. So, while Woody isn't every woman's dream man, there are plenty of ladies who understand perfectly what Diane saw in him.

Life with Woody

Life with a man who keeps a constant deathwatch can't possibly be a lark. But Diane denies that Woody's as grim a companion as he makes himself out to be. "Woody has a great capacity for joy," she says. "He's moved by things and he has a great sense of beauty. He's very sensitive and he has these feelings of guilt and anger and shame. Who's to say where it comes from, or why?"

Woody himself is very much involved in finding out where it comes from. *Interiors* focuses primarily on people's feelings about their own guilt, their sense of shame. His art invokes these feelings of inadequacy, of shame, of *mea culpa*. And yet, though he indicates that these negative emotions are intrinsic to the human condition, though he is enthralled by them to the point of near obsession, he offers no solution for their expulsion. We're stuck with this unfortunate baggage, he seems to say, and we can neither accept it nor forget about it. Perhaps we shouldn't even try.

Woody doesn't think much of happiness as a life aim. He even confesses to resenting the fact that so many people do accept having a good time as their goal. Recently, he told interviewer Dave Sheehan, "I have to admit that I really do still feel resentful about so many of my friends moving here to Los Angeles. They've been seduced by television and a life more pleasant than in New York City. And I, as you know, don't feel an aim in life is to be happy or to have nice weather or that kind of stuff. So I have a mild antipathy. If not New York, I would live in Paris. I would not want to live in a culture where I have to drive a car all the time to get places, and where there was a kind of relentless weather that was the same all the time, or where I couldn't jaywalk without thinking I'm going to have

There's no better way to learn how not to be conspicuous than by going out with Woody Allen.

Woody and Diane were wonderful together in
Annie Hall — maybe because so much of it was
based on their real relationship.

to explain it to somebody."

So Woody stays in New York and slyly
derides the Los Angeles mentality in his
movies. He has embraced the true New
York lifestyle (after all, he was born and
raised there). He lives in a penthouse on
Fifth Avenue, walks the streets unmolested
in his traditional "disguise" of slouchy
khaki hat, goes to the theater and the ballet,
peruses books and paintings in shops and
galleries, and, in general, has a much better
time than he would admit.

Here's the look that launched a thousand department store campaigns — Woody and Diane,
in her *Annie Hall* duds.

Diane has managed to make the transition to being a New Yorker, while retaining
her appreciation of some of the West
Coast's simpler joys. She, too, lives on New
York's East Side, and she can often be seen
shopping on Fifth Avenue, attending
museum shows, or just enjoying a stroll
down the streets in her long Annie Hall
skirts, hacking jackets, and dark leather
cowboy boots.

Her relationship with Woody has sur-
vived the test of time. They have managed,

as so few couples do, to go from being lovers to being friends without carrying ill-will along like an unwanted offspring. How have they done it? Diane gives much of the credit to Woody, to his passion for lasting attachments, to his sense of loyalty, to the plain and simple fact that "once you're his friend, that's it. You can call him any hour of the day or night, and he's there for you."

Just like their characters in *Annie Hall,* Woody and Diane broke up but never broke away from their tender, caring feelings for each other. Their relationship is in a category by itself. They aren't lovers, but they're more than friends. They're not like brother and sister, because they've been too much else to each other. They are encouragement to everyone who has ever loved another person and had to see it end, but wishes there was a way to remain friends. In *Annie Hall,* and in their own lives, Diane and Woody have said, "Yes, there is a way."

Since his affair with Diane ended, Woody hasn't been involved in a long romantic relationship with any other woman. He'd already been married twice when he met Diane, and it's typical of Woody that he's always spoken highly of both his ex-wives. He married his first wife, Harlene, when both were still in their teens. It was more a case of two kids wanting to be grown up and on their own than two people with a lasting basis for marriage. His second wife, actress Louise Lasser, co-starred with him in *Bananas,* then went on to achieve even greater fame on her own as the title star of the late-night television soap opera, *Mary Hartman,*

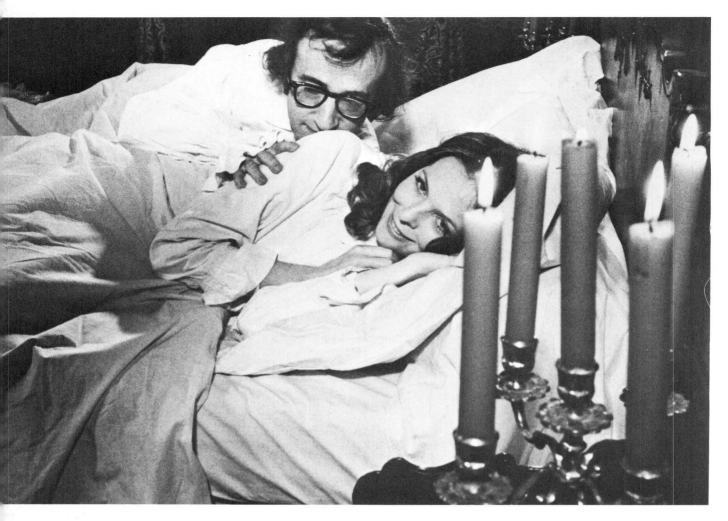

Love and Death, 1975. **This expansive Russian epic satirized everything from Bergman to Tolstoy.**

Mary Hartman. By the time he met Diane, Woody was marriage-shy. The two of them never got to the altar, and both have kept their personal feelings about marriage to themselves.

Diane, with her whimsical sense of humor and her heartfelt appreciation of a good laugh, seems to have managed to introduce an element of fun into Woody's life as no other woman has. Just as Annie lightened Alvy Singer's outlook in *Annie Hall*, Diane has helped Woody see the bright,

white spots amid all the black and the gray.

Diane, insouciant and refreshingly open, is always enthusiastic about any pursuit that catches her interest. She's not one to try to act blasé or to shrug off the most important things in her life with an "I couldn't care less" attitude. What she likes, she likes. What she wants, she longs for desperately. What she feels, she experiences fervently.

One of the interests in which she's immersed herself is photography. She's long

been interested in the photographic field, and, with a photographer for a mother, she received early encouragement in this sphere. Woody made use of her photographic bent in *Annie Hall.* In her real-life apartment the walls are covered with Diane's own prints, and several galleries are interested in showing her work. She approaches this avocation with the same earnestness that Woody exhibits when playing jazz.

Diane is also a devotee of the dance. She was undoubtedly a deciding factor (if not *the* deciding factor) in Woody's decision to study with the *grande dame* of modern dance, Martha Graham, in 1973. Today, it's still difficult to imagine Woody enjoying dance classes—and he admits the experience was less than his idea of heaven. "It was interesting but it wasn't fun," he says. "It was quite embarrassing for a thirty-eight-year-old person to buy a dance belt and leotards and sit in class. I didn't mind being there, but once you had to get up and

prance across the floor with the others and do the big, open steps, I couldn't make it. My sense of shame just overtook me."

Diane understands Woody's sense of shame. She has a well-developed sense of it herself, and it doesn't take much for her self-consciousness to push its way to the surface. She has never been entirely at ease with herself, and until recently she wouldn't even sit through her own movies because she felt uncomfortable watching herself on the screen.

Diane has always been the same way about her singing—the aspect of her career that is perhaps most precious to her. When she made her professional singing debut, at Greenwich Village's Reno Sweeney in 1975, she asked Woody not to come. She wouldn't have been at ease knowing he was watching her putting herself on the line that way.

But she needn't have worried. Coming into the spotlight in a simple black dress, unadorned, unsophisticated, and with a refreshing lack of pretension for a cabaret singer, Diane gently crooned old ballads in a manner akin to her singing "Seems Like Old Times" in *Annie Hall*. She even offered a few surprises, like her zany rendition of Randy Newman's "Last Night I Had a Dream," in which she supplied her own comically spooky "ghost" noises. She was an immediate success.

In *Annie Hall*, Diane sits unassumingly on a high stool in front of a microphone in a club very much like Reno Sweeney and croons her songs of love to Alvy Singer in one of the movie's most poignant moments. In real life, she was singing to a group of Manhattan sophisticates, all of whom liked her style just fine. When the reviews came out, most critics were favorably impressed with her simple, unaffected style and her clear, sweet voice. At the time, no one knew how difficult it had been for her to keep her composure. A close friend had just been killed in an accident, but Diane kept the news to herself and performed like a true pro.

Around Woody, Diane has always been able to shed her self-consciousness, perhaps because his sense of the Other watching and judging him is even stronger than hers, perhaps because he's always found her self-deprecating nature so endearing. All the characters Diane has played in Woody's movies have that air of apology, that gently derogatory attitude toward themselves that wins over viewers as much as it won over Woody when he met Diane.

Woody's love and admiration for Diane come through whenever he mentions her. He is passionately fond of her, happy to discuss her rather than himself. While others might call him the man who changed Diane Keaton's life, he's quick to point out what a tremendous influence she's had on him.

"She has an utterly spectacular visual sense," he says of Keaton. "I see many things today through her eyes, textures and forms I would never have seen without her. She showed me the beauty of the faces of old people. I'd never been sensitive to that before. And there's a certain warmth and poignance associated with young women that I never would have seen without her. She's increased my affection, feeling, and understanding for women in general."

In *Love and Death*, Diane's Sonia typifies the inept but lovable heroines of many of Woody's films.

Woody's changed attitude toward women is most evident in *Interiors*. The women in that film are three-dimensional, as interesting as (if not more interesting than) the men. *Interiors* is that rare instance in American cinema—a film in which most of the leading roles are played by women. He hasn't just given one woman a strong part and then cast the others in throwaway roles. And one aspect of what he has dealt with in the film—the importance of the mother's role—is surely a feminist consideration.

Critic Ross Wetzsteon of *The Village Voice* agrees that Diane has influenced Woody's feelings toward the opposite sex. In an article in *Ms.* magazine, he stated that up until *Annie Hall*, the women in Woody's movies had served only as "projections of male lust." And he added that *Annie Hall* was the first Woody Allen film to deal with what happened to two people *after* they went to bed together.

All of this isn't to say that Diane is the prime mover in Woody's increasing awareness of women as people. What is reflected in his films is the change taking place in American culture. Diane is the Late Seventies Woman, the woman who is coming into her own and examining her options with a seriousness and sense of purpose that, until recently, were considered male prerogatives.

Though others have perceived subtle misogynistic influences in Woody's work before *Annie Hall*, Diane has always appeared blissfully unaware of them. In addition to being one of her favorite people, Woody is one of her favorite directors. She admires his artistic sense of honor, his talent, his intellect. She is always pleased to announce that she'll be appearing in yet another Woody Allen film.

"I work with him a lot because I really like the parts," Diane says unhesitatingly and unapologetically. "And I'm comfortable with him. We're very good friends. I talk to him a lot, and we see each other every week. We laugh and share things. He's very good to his friends, he's always been tremendously encouraging to them, always giving them a big push."

Diane is one friend to whom Woody has always offered encouragement. And it's interesting to note that the biggest break he gave her was not as her lover but as her friend—when he wrote *Annie Hall* just for her.

Growing

In the years since Diane and Woody broke up, their friendship has continued to flourish. They keep in constant contact with each other. Even though her success has caused Diane's circle of friends to expand, Woody is still one of the core people in her life. If the phone rings in Diane's apartment, chances are it's Woody. If he's going to the Garden for a Knicks game, often as not Diane's by his side. If she's shopping on Fifty-seventh Street, one might spy that russet-haired figure slouching beside her. If he's sneaking into an East Side movie theater, hoping to catch a film unobserved, the lady in glasses by his side is most probably you-know-who.

Woody and Diane's relationship was too important to be shrugged off after the romance ended. It was important enough for the Best Picture of 1977 to have been written about it, and it was important enough to continue to this day.

Diane feels very close to *Annie Hall*, which is only natural since she's the star of it and since it represents a certain view of her, the view through Woody Allen's eyes.

"None of the facts in *Annie Hall* are true," Diane says, "but the essence of the characters and the relationship is pretty similar—their feeling, I mean, about each other. There was no problem with me acting inarticulate, you know, and sort of self-conscious and embarrassed and laughing a lot and so forth. The hard part was letting myself do it, without getting in my own way, you know, and ending up doing it off the top. I didn't want to stop myself from going all the way with it. I didn't want to put any stops on my reactions. I just wanted to do it as fully as I could."

Diane did it more fully than anyone else could have. After all, she was more familiar with the material than any other actress could possibly have been. Watching Annie

Hall, one gets the feeling that *this* was exactly what Diane was like when Woody met her. Diane is Annie, and Annie is Diane.

Diane was extraordinarily pleased with the film's reception, and with the enthusiasm for her part in it. She always thought it was an important movie, one with something for everybody. In fact, Diane thinks the film's universality is the main reason for its popularity. Practically everyone can relate to it on one level or another. "First," she explains, "it affects *couples* so much because everybody knows, I think, how difficult it is to have a relationship and to keep it alive and continuing. So there's a universal fact of life that says breaking up happens to everybody, so no one should feel like a failure when it does happen.

"Then, it's also sort of Pygmalion, you know. He teaches her and guides her, but then she goes off on her own when she finds the relationship becoming too insular, too confining, too negative, and so she proceeds out into her own life. But in the end they're still friends, they still like each other, and they know they can't go back to the way it once was. That's touching, you know, it's sort of bittersweet, the idea that you still have a lot of affection for this person but you both know that too much time and change has taken place. But life is time and change, and it just cannot always be worked out, no matter how much affection there may be. I personally feel that I want to have my own life and work and be with somebody who thinks of me as an equal, you know, and that's what's important for everybody."

Diane speaks of the plot in general terms, without relating it specifically to her relationship with Woody. Was he her Pygmalion? Did she find their personal relationship sometimes insular, confining, negative? She won't say. Though Diane speaks easily of her individual problems—her shyness, her inarticulateness, her lack of healthy ego—she is close-mouthed on the subject of her relationship with Woody. She'll quickly consent to discussing his talent, his great friendship, his interests, but when it comes to talking about what it was like living with such an eccentric genius or exactly why they decided to part, Diane keeps mum. Privacy is very important to her, especially about her emotional relationships. She has an old-fashioned respect for the confidences, fears, and love that are exchanged between two people. What happened between Diane and Woody, she rightly feels, is their business and their right to keep to themselves.

It's not unusual for Diane to sound as if she's putting herself down. She often says things like, "There was no problem with me acting inarticulate, you know, and sort of self-conscious and embarrassed and laughing a lot and so forth. . . ." She has always been ill at ease in social situations, and certainly she has never been able to relax around men. Even winning the Oscar hasn't given her the kind of confidence that would allow her to sweep into a room with a beaming smile of self-assurance. No matter how famous and successful she may become, it's difficult to imagine Diane without that "Oh, I hope they like me" look, that hesitant smile, that diffident aura

Although their romance is over, Diane and Woody remain the closest of friends.

Diane, flanked by a retiring Woody Allen and a hungry Michael Murphy, who also appeared in *Annie Hall*.

of doubt, that pleased beam of wonderment when she's accepted by her peers.

This self-conscious, embarrassed side of Diane comes through in all her work. Perhaps it is the essence of her personality. Fine-boned and delicate, there is more than a little bit of the fawn in her. Her hesitancy makes people want to embrace her, to help her. She wins over strangers by her sheer candor, by her startling lack of armor against the world. When she first began appearing on talk shows, viewers were amazed. Why, here was a Hollywood star who was just as intimidated and worried about saying the wrong thing to Johnny and Ed as the rest of us would be! She was as nervous and giddy about being on a TV talk show as the housewife from Albuquerque with the homemade barbeque sauce she's pushing. Diane's fans have always loved her for her weaknesses as well as for her strengths.

What is the source of Diane's insecurity? Even Woody is sometimes astounded by it, stating in objective surprise, "Diane is always totally surprised when people find her amusing. She is a natural comedienne, but she never quite believes she can do it."

Of course, we all know she *can* do it. She's hysterically funny, whether she's beaning someone on the head with a shoe, driving her car under the West Side Highway, or giving a twenty-first century cocktail party with Woody as her robot butler. She has no reason to doubt herself as an actress, in view of the awards and applause she's been steadily receiving over the past few years. But that's the way she is, and if she exuded self-confidence, well, then she wouldn't be Diane.

This unsureness—about her effect on other people, about her talent, about her future—colors every facet of Diane's life. "I'm very afraid," she admits. Afraid of what? Her answer is so simple that it's totally disarming. "Of life."

To help overcome her fears, she has been in analysis for more than five years, frequently seeing her analyst several times a week. Allen, who shows signs of becoming a lifetime analysand, influenced her decision to go into analysis, and it's a decision she has had no cause to regret. If anything, she appears to be more satisfied with the results of her analysis than Allen is with his.

Going into any kind of therapy or analysis is a big commitment, but Diane is not sorry she decided to make it. "It's a slow process, but I feel I've been helped," she says. "I feel like I'm more able to extend myself with people and that I'm not as threatened as I used to be."

Talking to anyone, much less a psychia-trist, isn't very easy for Diane. She's never glib. Her speech is punctuated by pauses, explanations, reconsiderations, asides, and nervous laughter. She describes herself as "more instinctive than verbal, more visual. I've gotten a little bit better at expressing myself through words, but I'm no great shakes."

Diane cares very much about words, though. She wants very much to make herself clear, to explain things in a precise manner, so that she won't be misunderstood. But she is not a brilliant conversationalist. She is a woman more comfortable with visual images than with words, and she uses words only to make those images and feelings known to others.

Her visual, nonverbal qualities hold great appeal for Woody, a man who lives so much in the world of words. Woody's prose pieces are erudite, even when they veer toward slapstick. He loves words and uses them well, whether he's writing about Metterling's laundry lists or aping the Hemingway and Stein styles in "A Twenties Memory." In his films, however, he often strives for the purely visual comedic approach of a Buster Keaton or a Chaplin. He seems to suspect that his love of words hamper him as a director. And some critics have accused Woody of sticking a joke into a script just for a laugh rather than because it fits into the rest of the dialogue.

Super-literacy is dangerous for a filmmaker. Sometimes the actors in *Interiors* sound more like talking metaphors in an expressionistic short story than like dramatic characters in a movie.

Diane possesses a warm emotionality that draws more cerebral types to her. Her

Overleaf: When Woody escorted First Lady Betty Ford to the ballet, his real date was Diane. He arrived with her, then joined Mrs. Ford inside.

© Robin Platzer, Images

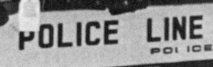

feelings are intense and close to the surface. Her honesty and candor keep her on the level with her friends. It is well nigh impossible for her *not* to tell someone exactly what's on her mind, although if it's not particularly pleasant or complimentary, she'll have a hard time getting it out and will do her best to be gentle about it.

The loyalty with which Diane credits Woody applies to her as well. Her friendships are lasting and important to her. She has stayed with the same manager, Arlene Rothberg, for almost eight years, and they are friends as well as business associates. At the Academy Awards, she brought a date, but she also made sure her mother and sister Dorrie could accompany her.

The real attraction of Diane is that she's just plain *nice*. Her special breed of charm is hard to resist. In her eagerness to please, her undisguised vulnerability, her hesitant and hopeful smile, we see the childlike, easily wounded, wondrously believing side of ourselves. Diane doesn't emanate the squeaky-clean "goodness" of a Marie Osmond or a Debby Boone, but her kind of goodness is more appealing to sophisticated audiences. She doesn't pretend to be a Madonna or a Sister of Mercy, but we believe in her niceness and her ability to care about people more than we might if she seemed too good to be true. She's a very *human* person, even to those who don't know her. It is her genuineness, her lack of masks—her very ordinariness—that make her so unique.

Diane still feels shy around other stars, even contemporaries like Henry Winkler.

New Challenges

Deep down, we all have moments when we feel like a child playing grown-up. There's something about Diane Keaton that taps directly into that part of our consciousness. She always seems a bit like a child playing dress-up.

"Dress-up" is an apt term for it, because Diane's "eclectic" wardrobe is like the clothes a child picks out when playing house. There's something crazily adorable about Diane's fashion taste, something that's grabbed the eye of the rest of the world and made the Keaton look one of the most "in."

Most people think Diane adapted her present wardrobe from the clothes she wore in *Annie Hall*, but she was dressing like Annie before any of the rest of us knew who Annie Hall was.

If you look at old photographs of Diane, you'll see that she was wearing men's-wear tuxedo suits back in the early seventies, and that she was mixing and matching styles quixotically long before it was a fashion trend. The "Annie Hall look" is very much the "Diane Keaton look."

All Diane's clothes seem a little too big on her five-foot-seven, 115-pound, small-boned frame. In her baggy pants, tweed suits, or oversized gauzy dresses, she always seems frail and slight inside the cocoon of her fabric. Her auburn hair tends toward the unkempt; with or without glasses, her hazel eyes appear myopic; her whole being is usually suffused with an air of slightly frazzled bewilderment.

The unusual blending of Diane's clothes gives her a childlike quality. No matter what the occasion, she's never quite dressed up enough to seem like an adult. A sophisticated long gown would undoubtedly change her image. As it is, she always appears to be in costume, which suits her

While the world may picture Diane today in her thrift-shop *Annie Hall* duds, in *Sleeper* she displayed more extravagant fashion with ease and flair.

less-than-ideal self-image. If she doesn't attempt to be a *femme fatale*, then no one can ever accuse her of failing to pull it off. Her attractiveness is enhanced by her funky clothes because she seems like a fairy princess dressed in tatters.

Diane's little-girl look fits in perfectly with Woody's views on comedy. If it's true, as he says, that "when you do comedy, you're not sitting at the grown-ups' table, you're sitting at the children's table," then no one could be better at comedy than Diane. Like the new girl in town on the first day of school, she never seems certain that she's in the right seat.

In reality, of course, Diane has more than earned her adult credentials by playing the lead in the emotionally harrowing *Looking for Mr. Goodbar*. Though the film gathered mixed notices from critics—who felt it was either dramatically powerful or cheaply sensationalistic, who credited it with exploring the violence inherent in today's singles scene or who castigated the filmmakers for exploiting an ugliness best left ignored—no one had harsh words for Diane. Her performance as Teresa Dunn, devoted schoolteacher by day and bar prowler by night, was riveting.

The choice of Diane Keaton for the lead role came as a surprise to most moviegoers. The Terry Dunn of Judith Rossner's best-selling novel wasn't at all like Diane. She was a tough cripple who hid in her shell, too defensive and self-destructive to be reached. But Richard Brooks's version of Teresa Dunn was a more vulnerable creature, much more like the girl in the real-life murder case on which *Looking for Mr. Goodbar* was based.

The director wanted a sympathetic heroine, one with whom the audience would identify. Diane's presence changed the film so that it wasn't the same story as the book's. In the book, Terry Dunn was a woman unconsciously seeking her own destruction, primed for disaster from early childhood. She meets a young man who might have been harmless had he not come into contact with the death wish of Terry Dunn. In the movie, Brooks played up the big-city dangers, the allure and evil of the singles bar scene. His Terry Dunn is a lovely, vibrant young woman brought down more by chance than by her own unconscious manipulations.

Diane accepted the part because it was a plum role for an actress. It was also a challenge and an opportunity to do something vastly different from anything she'd tried before. Never before had she been offered the chance to portray a character with such varied shadings, such depth, such tragic dimensions. She couldn't have picked a better role with which to break away from Woody's company of players and establish herself as an actress in her own right. It was a role that took guts, endurance, and awesome talent.

In signing to direct *Looking for Mr. Goodbar*, Brooks made enormous concessions for the freedom to do the movie his way. Regardless of how anyone feels about the film, it was made with dedication and total involvement. Brooks believed in the movie, and he believed in Diane. And it's greatly to his credit as a director that he got an incredible performance out of her, one that both illuminated the tawdriness of the story and redeemed it of that same gratuitous tawdriness.

Though Brooks wanted Diane for the

Diane's interest in clothes leads her to fashion shows. Here she checks out a Ralph Lauren collection with Candice Bergen and writer Joel Schumakher.

role, he was not certain of her ability to descend into the depths of depravity and despair along with Terry Dunn. He says, "I never knew she could play the role for sure—I knew she could do half of it, the schoolteacher scenes—and she didn't seem to know for sure, either. But she has tremendous range, which we didn't know about. She is not as fragile as she appears. She's shy, but she's got stainless steel inside of her. She doesn't break easily. She doesn't have a high opinion of herself, but she's got a lot of guts. And she's tough. She is tough internally."

Tough. Yes, Diane can be tough. But on the set of *Goodbar*, her insecurity communicated itself, as always. Her director sensed that from the start—witness his remark that Diane didn't "have a high opinion of herself." What was really to impress Brooks was the way in which Diane could channel her lack of self-confidence, her self-doubts, even her low self-esteem, into the character and life of Teresa Dunn and

Frank Edwards, Fotos International/Pictorial Parade

Diane, as Teresa Dunn, courted disaster and found death in *Looking for Mr. Goodbar*.

give the performance of her career.

Like any gifted actress, Diane used facets of her own personality to get inside Terry Dunn's skin. And she managed to transform herself into the character in a way, and to a degree, that another actress might have found impossible. Diane *became* Terry Dunn on the screen. And she did it so well because she could tap into her own consciousness to understand the forces that motivated the character she was portraying. Diane's no Terry Dunn, but she

Left: *Goodbar* was a wonderful showcase for Diane. It gave her the chance to prove she could do serious acting.

could use her own sense of guilt and shame to get inside the role. Perhaps she couldn't accept the events of Teresa Dunn's short life, but she could comprehend and identify with the feelings, and for Diane, feelings are the keys that unlock all the doors.

As far as toughness is concerned, Diane proved herself to be made of pretty stern stuff. She was an unstinting trouper in a grueling role. She even shrugged off the broken rib she got when she took a bad fall during a fight scene with actor Richard

Gere. Diane was quick to let everyone know that it wasn't Gere's fault she'd gotten hurt. She knew how to fall, and she should have known better than to fall the way she had. On the set of *Looking for Mr. Goodbar,* Diane carried herself like a true professional. She never for a minute expected star treatment.

The role was a real departure for her. Not only had she never played a part like that of Teresa Dunn before, but the character was also a far cry from the real Diane. She never was the type to haunt singles bars or to indiscriminately seek out strange men. When Diane says frankly, "I've never picked up a man in my life," you *know* she means it.

Sensitive as she is, Diane could empathize greatly with Terry's need for love and her denial of that need. As a single woman, Diane understands what it's like for a woman living alone in New York City.

At the same time, Terry frightened her. Diane got so deeply involved in Terry Dunn's complex, convoluted personality that, like Ann-Margret during the filming of *Carnal Knowledge,* she sometimes found it almost impossible to escape from her character. Diane would find herself growing depressed off the set, overwhelmed by Terry Dunn's sense of despair, despondent over the grim tale she had to live with day after day. Toward the end of the filming, it got harder and harder for her to shrug off the bleakness at the core of Teresa Dunn's personality. Even after she'd left the studio for the day, the grimness would hang on.

At the same time, Diane found out a lot about the good side of her own personality by learning about the Terry Dunns of the world. The very neuroticism of the part made Diane more aware of her own emotional healthiness. She had never been driven to promiscuous sex, to bar-hopping, to trying to blot out reality. She had always been able to channel her energies and her drives in constructive directions. All in all, *Looking for Mr. Goodbar* was a cathartic experience for her, one that made her grow as an actress and as a person.

Perhaps because the role was so suffocating, so stifling emotionally, Diane found the physical aspects of it a welcome release. She enjoyed the knockdown, drag-out fights, the roughhousing, the slugging and wrestling. Her release through these battles wasn't the masochistic satisfaction Terry Dunn enjoyed, however. Instead, she found the physical confrontations a way of dealing with the pent-up energy she had accumulated in such an intense role. Being an actor is much more than being a machine for spouting words. It's a very physical occupation, and any good performer has a body that's been strenuously trained. Few of Diane's role have allowed her to express herself as an actress in this directly physical manner. So, in this area, *Goodbar* allowed her to stretch herself and test herself. She rose to the challenge and enjoyed it all the more.

Diane loved being able to play a part that had so many nuances. She liked portraying someone who was complicated, who was real, whose function in a film was more than to get some laughs. "I want parts with some sense of what life is about," she told the *New York Post* not long ago, "all the anxieties there are, the problems. That

Designer Theodora Van Runkle appreciates Diane's fashion sense, even when Diane wears simple outfits.

Frank Edwards, Fotos International/Pictorial Parade

doesn't exclude comedy, needless to say. Not all knit-brow serious, please. But it's so difficult to do something well, movies particularly, because there are so many things involved that you'd better be trying to do something good from the beginning. And when it works, it's wonderful."

It worked for Diane in *Looking for Mr. Goodbar*. That movie filled all her requirements. It dealt boldly with modern-day anxieties, with the very real problems of urban living. It gave Diane a part that considered very starkly what life is about.

Richard Brooks's doubts about Diane's ability to handle the role dissolved more and more with each day of shooting. He gained great respect for her as an actress, as a woman, and as a human being. By the time filming on the picture had concluded, he was stunned by her talent, dedication, and screen presence. He knew he had a real live star on his hands, and he knew she had done incredible things for his film.

"We shot for seventy-six days," he says, "of which Diane shot seventy-six days. There's no scene in the picture she's not a party to—except one, and that runs about a minute—but suddenly she's not there, and the audience starts thinking 'something's happening here' without really knowing what's going to happen.''

One of the things about *Goodbar* that was most difficult for Diane was the shooting of the nude scenes. She had never done one before, and she'd always taken it for granted that she'd *never* be called upon to do one. Now she was faced with taking off her clothes in front of the camera because it was a necessary act if the movie's story line was to be accepted as real.

It wasn't easy for Diane to agree to shed her clothes. She's such a private person, and certainly nothing is less private than letting the world gaze upon your naked body. She was very concerned and even spent several sessions discussing her fears and apprehensions with her analyst before finally agreeing to do the scenes.

Brooks tried to help her as much as he could. On the days when Diane did her nude scenes, he closed the set to everyone except those technicians who absolutely had to be there. He understood and accepted the fact that she was more sensitive about throwing off her clothes in front of a group of technicians than many other actresses would be. And he did everything in his power to help her relax.

Diane made up her mind that the nude scenes were a job she had to do to maintain the integrity of her role. She had agreed to them when she'd agreed to do the movie, and she realized that the bedroom scenes were of primary importance in a film with a sexual theme. So Diane overcame her doubts and her objections. She knew what she had to do and she did it well. She didn't enjoy those scenes—they were painful for her to do—but she did them to the best of her ability in the name of a good

performance. And that performance has surely been one of the strongest of her career to date.

One person who had only raves about Diane's work in *Looking for Mr. Goodbar* is her former mentor Allen. Woody was knocked out by Diane's acting in the film. He thought she did a wonderful job without his hand to guide her, and he enthused to *New York Times* writer Guy Flatley, "Of course, you know I'm prejudiced, but I think she is absolutely sensational in it. But that's something I've always known about Diane. If in some small way, I've contributed to bringing her to the attention of the filmgoing public, that's enough for me. It satisfies me more than anything else I've done in films.''

That's probably the greatest compliment Woody could have paid Diane—to say that her success satisfies him as much as anything else in his career—and one can be sure it came from the heart. Woody has long been one of Diane's staunchest supporters. He has always encouraged her to go out on her own, to develop her potential, to try the toughest challenges. A weaker man might have undermined Diane's confidence, tried to get her to remain one of his personal players, kept her on the sidelines as a special property of his own.

And Woody is responsible in more than just "some small way" for bringing Diane to the attention of the filmgoing public—not to mention the big studios and other important directors. Woody helped groom Diane for success, and no one could be more pleased than he with her stardom today.

Diane and Warren Beatty seem to enjoy the same easy rapport that marked Diane's relationship with Woody.

Off stage

No one can praise Diane Keaton's acting without giving Woody Allen credit for his teaching and direction. This is certainly evident in *Interiors*, where, under Woody's coaching, Diane has turned in the most mature, developed performance of her career.

A good director doesn't just move people around like pawns on his own private chessboard. He is also a tutor. He makes actors aware of their individual gifts. He instructs them in the craft of acting. He helps them make use of their bodies as instruments to convey emotions. Diane's excellent use of all her skills is a credit to Woody as a director and an instructor. She's used everything he's taught her over the years to become a better actress.

Woody makes no bones about the fact that the Diane Keaton character in *Interiors* is close to his own persona. It's not really unusual that he would choose a woman he knows so well to play his alter ego in a film in which he does not appear. But Woody says that he also identifies in part with the characters played by the other actors in his film—Marybeth Hurt, Geraldine Page, Sam Waterston, Richard Jordan, Maureen Stapleton, and Kristen Griffith.

Woody has always been appreciative of the scope of Diane's talents. He admired her for her decision to do *Looking for Mr. Goodbar* because he knew that the role, and the seriousness of the subject matter, posed both a challenge and a risk for her. Woody, serious man that he is, respects the need to do something that stretches one's limits, especially if that something represents a break from comedy.

Perhaps Diane's desire to do a serious film like *Goodbar* was in part inspired by Woody's own attitude about the difference between serious drama and comedy. As he

Diane, with first Oscar winner Janet Gaynor, wasn't blasé about winning her Academy Award. She was ecstatic.

told *Newsweek*'s Jack Kroll, "When you do comedy, you're not sitting at the grown-ups' table, you're sitting at the children's table." With *Interiors*, he changed tables, making a deliberate jump from comedy to tragedy. What made the jump so startling was that he had long been considered America's best director of comedy.

Diane likes being pushed, being stretched, having to extend herself. Like Woody, she wants to be at the grown-ups' table, wants to do the hard parts, the serious stuff. Both she and Woody have the overachiever's drive, though Diane, California girl that she is, seems to find it easier to throw off the cloak of hard work and relax and have a good time. Still, like Woody, she tries not to allow herself to become overly satisfied with anything she's done. She'd rather rise to the next challenge, take the next hurdle, continue to push herself and to follow every new avenue open to her.

This is why Diane prefers living in New York to moving back to the West Coast. The West Coast offers a calmer, more idyllic situation, but a mellow, laid-back lifestyle is exactly what Diane wants to avoid. "New York pushes me a little harder," she reveals. "I like that. Maybe I don't trust myself enough even now. I like being tested. I think it's good for me."

Diane's not being tested these days by living in poverty. Her New York apartment is on East Sixty-eighth Street, in a tree-filled, manicured area that's the bastion of Manhattan's old money. Her two-bedroom apartment is a far cry from that tub-in-the-kitchen Bohemian haunt she occupied back in the days of *Hair*.

The building itself is Art Deco, old, sturdy, and prestigious. The inside of the apartment is more *Annie Hall*-ish. The rooms are sparsely furnished, but furnished in good modern taste. It's all very bright and airy, with a feeling of openness that's hard to come by in the middle of Manhattan. The walls are covered with Diane's own black-and-white photographs, much like her apartment in *Annie Hall*. There's an abundance of green plants, making the apartment a clean, sparkling oasis in the middle of a bustling city.

Diane currently lives there alone except for the company of her two cats. She's named one of them Buster as a tongue-in-cheek answer to all the people who ask her if she's any relation to the late comedian and filmmaker Buster Keaton. Actually, she isn't, but she seems to get a kick out of the mistake. (When she was performing at Reno Sweeney, her repertoire included "Daddy Was a Vaudeville Man.")

One of the most important areas of Diane's apartment is the darkroom she had installed to perfect her skills as a photographer. The apartment could belong to a photographer as easily as to an actress. It's simple and functional, expensively fixed up, but far from luxurious.

Diane cares more for function than for luxury. It's because of this attitude that her success hasn't especially changed her life. She's not the type of woman to be concerned with diamonds or furs or yachts so much as she is with work, friends, and simple pleasures. She's determined not to become a different person, and to that effect, she's being very careful about what she does next. She considers every step of

Interiors, **1978. Woody Allen's first completely serious dramatic film both surprised and impressed the critics and the public. Here, Diane Keaton appears with co-star Marybeth Hurt.**

her career, and her life, from all the angles before making a decision. When Diane Keaton does something, you may be sure it isn't on the spur of the moment.

Instead of taking her work for granted now that she's a success, Diane is giving it more thought than ever. Now that she can pick and choose her parts, she wants to get involved only in projects she considers worthy of her talents.

"Oh, yes," she told the *New York Post* in January 1978, "the scripts are rolling in, but I don't want to get carried away. I just concern myself with doing as well as I can with the work. Otherwise, it gets very confusing.

"It's been a strange and wonderful year, but I feel slightly removed from it all. I've always thought of acting as an art to be practiced. But I'd be a fool to say the idea of receiving attention isn't kind of interesting. When you're doing it, that's what matters. Getting there, and being famous, are the hard parts."

She's accomplished the hard parts now. She's there. She's famous. Now it's up to her to decide what to do with her career, what's the next best move along the road.

Diane's desire to be a singer is still strong. She continues to study voice and there's talk of a record contract. The dream that was in her heart when she sang to the moon as a five year old is still there. "What really thrilled me about *Annie Hall*," she's confessed, "was that I was able to sing in it."

Singer Nick Holmes, who appeared on the bill with Diane when she sang at Reno Sweeney, remembers that she struck him as someone not particularly interested in music. She never gave a hint of the importance of singing in her life.

"I thought she was doing it more for something new to do than because she had any driving ambition to be a singer," Holmes recalls. And he remembers that she never hung around the bar after the last show. As soon as she was finished performing, she packed up and went home.

When Diane did have to sit around—in the dressing room between shows—it was movies that were on her mind. She got a kick out of curling up and playing movie games with Nick and her musical conductor. One of her favorites was the one where one person names a movie, the next person names an actor in that movie, the next person names a different movie with that actor in it, the first person then has to name another actor in the new movie, and so on.

Diane was happier playing these games than she was having heavy conversations. "I really liked her, and I always felt sure she was doing something to maintain her

The three sisters in *Interiors*: Diane Keaton, Kristin Griffith, and Marybeth Hurt.

privacy. She never came off it," Holmes says. "I don't think she wanted many people to know her. You know, she'd be coy enough to be unbelievable, but it was always attractive enough that you didn't care if it was an act. And I never thought she herself was that aware that she was doing it, which made it even more attractive. I'd describe her as just being very private."

It's not as easy for Diane to maintain that privacy now that she's beat out Shirley MacLaine (*The Turning Point*), Jane Fonda (*Julia*), Anne Bancroft (*The Turning Point*), and Marsha Mason (*The Goodbye Girl*) for the Best Actress Award in the Oscars race. That's the kind of thing that does tend to change one's life a bit and make people more interested.

Diane wasn't blasé about the Oscar. She showed up at the Awards ceremony with a perky new hairdo, an upsweep of soft curls, and wearing a long skirt and tweedy jacket, her face aglow with the joy of being nominated. When her name was called out as winner, she looked stunned, disbelieving, and just plain thrilled. And she was. But in spite of her pleasure at being recognized, Diane doesn't want that little gold statuette to gain control over her life. She wants to remain as much like she was before as possible. Frankly, she can't imagine why such a thing *should* make her any different.

When David Sheehan asked her, before the Oscars presentation, if she felt that winning the Oscar wouldn't change her in any way, Diane answered thoughtfully, "Wouldn't change me? Well, I don't know. I don't think so. I guess in the same sense that anything that happens in your life has

Richard Jordan played Diane's novelist husband in *Interiors*.

some effect on you. But, I mean, I don't think it would make a radical change. I mean, I don't think that I'm going to show up in a gown and a tiara from then on and be Mrs. Elegant."

So far Diane has lived up to her own prediction. The Academy Award doesn't appear to have changed her, and it certainly hasn't changed her personal style. She thinks that she responds to such things in a different way than someone from the East Coast would.

"I'm a Southern California girl," she says. "My conditioning was different. When I was a kid, the family used to gather around every year watching the Academy Awards. Remember when Bob Hope used

per of them all, the Best Picture award.

Nor did *Annie Hall* clean up only at the Oscars. It also won the National Society of Film Critics and the New York Film Critics Circle awards as the best film of 1977. Not bad for a film many suspected would go unrewarded.

Why would people think that *Annie Hall*'s excellence might go unrecognized at the Academy Awards? Certainly not because people didn't like it—the film got unanimously good reviews and played to packed houses. The problem was Woody and his crew's anti-Hollywood image. The old guard in Hollywood saw them as rebels who were against everything the Awards stood for. And Woody himself has remarked that he finds the Awards unfair and disapproves of the competition they encourage among actors, writers, and filmmakers.

Though Diane never personally spoke out against the Awards, many felt that she would be· hurt by her association with Woody and by the fact that *Annie Hall* was his picture. Her boosters feared she would have to carry the onus of Woody's antiestablishment sentiments. The consensus was that Diane would lose the Best Actress Award to someone more "acceptable" to the Academy, someone like Anne Bancroft (considered the most likely to win the race) or Shirley MacLaine.

Woody didn't even bother to attend the Awards show in California. But Diane wouldn't have missed it for the world, and showed up with her date, her mother, and her sister to cheer her on. Writer Marshall Brickman appeared to be every bit as pleased with his Oscar as Diane was with

to host them? God, I mean, it was like watching a big family event—are you kidding?—the suspense of who was going to win and all that stuff. So in terms of, like, my background, of course the Oscars have a certain kind of meaning to me. But I don't know what it means in terms of what it makes you if you win. You know what I mean? I mean, I don't think it suddenly gives your life value, you know?"

Annie Hall gathered awards like a gardener passing through a field plucking roses. Besides Diane's Oscar as Best Actress, the film won three other Academy Awards: one for Woody as Best Director, one for Woody and Marshall Brickman as Best Original Screenplay, and the big bop-

hers. Both he and Diane thanked the conspicuously absent Woody in their acceptance speeches.

That night Woody played his usual Monday night date with his jazz group back at Michael's Pub in New York. He went to bed without knowing he'd won, and, he says, without even checking the news for the results out of simple curiosity.

"I was very surprised," he said afterward. "I felt good for Diane because she wanted to go and wanted to win. My friend Marshall had a very nice time and my producer Jack Rollins had a very nice time. But I'm anhedonic," he explained, referring to the condition he describes as an inability to enjoy oneself.

It's hard to imagine anyone caring that little about whether or not he wins an Academy Award! Still, it fits in with Woody's character that he would not care whether or not he won, or even want to know *if* he'd won. Like all other long-term states of being, anhedonia calls for a certain commitment on the part of the victim.

But Diane, while not a hedonist, isn't anhedonic in the slightest. She wanted to be there, and she wanted to win. And now that she has, she wants to enjoy every wonderful minute of her success.

Diane doesn't want anything to change her life, but in a very positive way, something already has. Whether it's winning the Oscar or her analysis or growing older or the ego boost her newfound success has given her, Diane Kaaton is at last truly coming into her own. To the rest of the world, she's now one of the Beautiful People. And surprisingly, it looks as if Diane's got enough self-confidence now to actually believe it!

Before winning 1977's Best Actress Oscar, Diane chatted with her competitor Jane Fonda and Jane's son, Tracy Hayden.

A New Romance

On the surface, Diane's life doesn't seem to have changed all that much since winning the Academy Award. She still lives in the same apartment. She still has the same friends. She's still running around town in her long skirts and hacking jackets and cowboy boots. She is still shy and seems surprised when people gush over how great she is.

Her reputation as an actress has, of course, changed greatly. People are sitting up and taking notice of her, especially since the release of *Interiors*. She's no longer just "that girl who's in all the Woody Allen movies." She's a star, a bona fide celebrity of the highest order. Her acceptance as a serious actress is the icing on the cake, typified by the impressive reviews she's received for *Interiors*, in which she plays Renata, the serious poet tormented by her self-doubt and unfulfilled relationships.

Diane has just finished filming yet another movie with Woody, this time a comedy, which Woody reveals is about his usual theme—"the inability to function in contemporary society."

Many of her fans would like to see Diane's relationship with Woody take off again, but it doesn't appear that it will. Making *Annie Hall* didn't spark a romantic renewal between the two. Instead, the experience cemented the theme Woody was dealing with in that film—when two people end an affair they can remain friends, but friends are what they will remain. Diane and Woody's relationship has gone through many changes over the years, and in most ways, it's stronger now than ever. But it's evolved into a different kind of relationship from what it was at the start. It's metamorphosed into an amazingly close tie that nothing can destroy. Woody and Diane have learned from each other and each has become more like the other.

Woody has learned from Diane how to see things he had never seen before, and Diane has learned a lot intellectually from Woody.

Annie Hall seemed to tie up the loose ends of their relationship and left Diane free to go on to other love affairs. In making her the star of that film, Woody helped her to become independent.

For the first time in a very long while, Diane is seeing a new man—and spending less time with Woody. And the new man is certainly a catch for the girl who never got the handsome basketball players back in high school. Warren Beatty was a high-school football star, but he's always been the handsomest of the handsome. He's every girl's dream man, and Diane is the woman he's spending most of his time with these days.

On the surface, these two might seem an unlikely pair, but in reality, Diane and Warren have a lot in common. Like Diane, Warren moved to New York shortly after high school to pursue an acting career, and, like her, he took odd jobs to support himself until he started getting steady work as an actor. He also got his start on the Broadway stage and made the transition to movies.

Warren is like Diane in more ways than just professionally. For one thing, he's a very private person, and, at forty-two, he has every intention of remaining that way. He appreciates Diane's reticence about discussing things she holds near and dear.

In a recent interview with *Time*, Warren said, "I have never talked about my personal relationships—with women, my sister, my parents—because these are impor-

tant people to me. I don't want to hurt them by discussing them in public. As for my love life, I can't control what others say about it; it is what it is. I know that movie actors are overrewarded in our society, and that the press has to cut people like me down to size. So they come up with all sorts of wild things. They make me into an insane eccentric with an incredible fear of losing my youth, who lives in a bomb shelter, who contemplates or is going through plastic surgery, who has devastating relationships with women. It goes through cycles. First they say that women like me too much; then that women don't like me at all; then that they like me too much again. Somewhere along the way they say I secretly like men—but then that men don't like me! I'm old. I'm young. I'm intelligent. I'm stupid. My tide goes in and out."

Like Warren, Diane has always abhorred this kind of gossip, but so far she's been able to avoid it better than he has. After all, Diane has never been a sex symbol, nor has she been around as long as Warren has. But her romantic link with someone as newsworthy as Warren is making everyone take more interest in her. Coupled with winning the Oscar, her relationship with Beatty is guaranteed to give her a fast lesson in the fickleness of the public and the elusiveness of anonymity.

Warren is often painted as the Playboy of the Western World, a man who spends most of his time calling chicks on the phone and hopping trans-Atlantic jets to get close to the action. The truth is that Beatty is a very complex man who enjoys solitude and peace as much as he enjoys

She says she never gets handsome men, but even Diane would have to admit you can't find men much better looking than Warren Beatty.

hobnobbing with the jet set.

Though Warren is a sought-after guest at most show business parties, he's not a big party guy, and when he does show up, he can usually be found talking business quietly in a corner instead of regaling the girls with stories or otherwise promoting himself. Beatty is a very astute businessman, and while business claims more of his time than pleasure, he's managed very adroitly to combine the two.

When Warren is seen dining out at places like Mr. Chow or the Bistro in Los Angeles, chances are he's on movie business rather than the Hollywood social whirl. He goes from one business discussion to another, and if he can combine dining with talking facts and figures, so much the better. He's certainly no gourmet, and he'd just as soon get his business done while he eats lunch or dinner. Nowadays Warren sees himself first and foremost as a producer, and the success of both *Shampoo* and *Heaven Can Wait* shows that he knows exactly what he's doing.

Diane appreciates the serious side of Warren. And, of course, after Woody, no one could possibly seem all that serious! Still, through her relationship with Warren, she's learning what she never got a chance to understand in high school—that great-looking guys have the same goals and problems as everyone else. Now that she's gotten to know Warren, she sees him as a fascinating, multifaceted man, not just another handsome guy. It's been a good experience for her.

Diane and Warren both prefer quiet evenings at the movies or the theater to dancing the night away at Studio 54. Both are great walkers who prowl the streets of Manhattan for hours on end. Both would rather walk down the street to buy apricot brandy ice-cream cones than fly to Cannes for rounds of film festival parties. Warren may be more sophisticated than Diane, but he's not more pretentious. He's happiest having a quiet time with a few close friends, and so is Diane.

Another trait Warren shares with Diane is his thirst for knowledge, his quest for education. His Los Angeles apartment is always cluttered with books and newspapers. Warren is a big believer in self-education; if any subject catches his fancy, he'll read everything he can on it. He's as much an adherent of the "stretch yourself and grow" philosophy as are Woody and Diane. He never wants to learn a little bit about anything—he wants to learn it all.

It's not difficult to see what attracted Warren to such a lovely, spontaneous woman as Diane. He's always loved women in general, and his name has been linked with the best of them—from Natalie Wood to Joan Collins to Leslie Caron to Joni Mitchell to Julie Christie to Michelle Phillips. Physically, Diane is certainly his type, long-limbed and slender, with delicate curves, a fine-boned face, and beautiful eyes. Like Warren, she comes from a well-to-do non-show-business family (his father was a school principal) and had a typically middle-class childhood.

Diane isn't much like Warren's other women in personality, but her tentativeness and vulnerability must hold great appeal for him. In his world, the high-powered Hollywood world, Warren doesn't meet many women who are as unaffected

This is a rare photo indeed — of Diane kicking up her heels and dancing at one of the parties she rarely attends.

and down to earth as Diane. Since she's always refused to live in Los Angeles, she's never assumed the Tinseltown shallowness of so many performers. (This shallowness really is common; it's not the figment of the imaginations of snappy-talking gossip mongers.) The special seriousness of Diane appeals to Warren. She's not a bubble-headed young starlet. She's a mature, aware actress. She's lived long enough to know what she wants out of life, and she understands the film business.

At the same time, Diane isn't a dyed-in-the-wool career woman. She's soft and feminine. She enjoys having a man around. In spite of the fact that she's a private person, she wants to share her life with a man. As she told Gene Shalit, "Ideally, I would like to have my privacy but also to be with somebody."

If that sounds like asking for the impossible, it isn't. As a matter of fact, Beatty has often admitted to feeling the same way. Even when he set up housekeeping with Michelle Phillips and her daughter China in the house he purchased on Los Angeles's secluded Mulholland Drive, he retained his bachelor apartment at the Beverly Wilshire Hotel so that he could have a little nook to himself when he felt the need to be alone.

Diane thinks it's important in any relationship to retain one's own privacy and to respect the other person's separateness. She thinks that the answer to a successful relationship is "separate rooms, you know, where you can go and do your work. I need to be by myself," she explains. "But I love to share time with somebody I trust and like and care for. I like the idea of being

Diane and Warren both prefer quiet walks and private evenings to star-studded Hollywood parties.

© Robin Platzer, Images

© Robin Platzer, Images

with one person for a lifetime but I don't know if I can do that. I have no history of it."

Diane is more open than ever to the idea of serious romantic involvement, and, indeed, she's now in an ideal position to form a serious attachment. She's established herself in her career after years of hard work and diligence. She has learned a great deal about herself and how she functions through psychoanalysis. Her new-found fame and success have buoyed her self-confidence, and, most of all, she is finally beginning to enjoy her life fully. Lately, her world has been beautiful. Sharing it with someone special would make it all the more beautiful.

Right now, everything points in the direction of Warren and Diane doing a film together. In *Heaven Can Wait*, Warren has shown that he's got a good grasp of comedy. This would be the perfect time for him to concentrate on cashing in on that comedic bent. And if he does decide to do a lighthearted movie, who could be better suited to play opposite him than Diane, who's an old pro at comedy?

Even if Warren were interested in producing and starring in a serious motion picture, Diane would be an ideal choice for his leading lady. She's a definite box-office draw now, and she and Beatty would be magical on the screen together.

For Diane, that would mean entering into a new relationship much like the one she shared with Woody for so long. She would be mixing business and plea-sure—working full-time with a man she's also dating. Some women would feel hemmed in by this kind of continuity; Diane seems to thrive on it.

But then, Diane is not, never has been, and never will be like anyone else. She's a little bit like everybody, but she's very much herself. She came from vapid Southern Clifornia to the intellectual salons of New York, and she's shown over the years that she's more than a flash in the pan. Too often, she belittles her own ability, but she has a core of steel and the courage to stand by her convictions. Whether it was refusing to strip in *Hair* or defying typecasting by signing to star in *Looking for Mr. Goodbar*, Diane has always done what she felt was best for herself. And once she makes up her mind to do something, she sticks by it.

Her low-profile iconoclasm has served her well. She's become one of the most popular, respected female stars in America. She's single-handedly started a fashion trend that's sweeping Europe with the same verve as America. She's being talked about and watched and copied and praised. She's a hot property, a trend-setter, a celebrity, a photographer, a wonderful actress.

Things have never looked brighter for Diane Keaton. There's no doubt now that she's going to be around for a long, long time. After all, she's a genuine star. And the nicest thing is that she's not impressed by her new status. She thinks it's all just sort of, well, la-di-da.